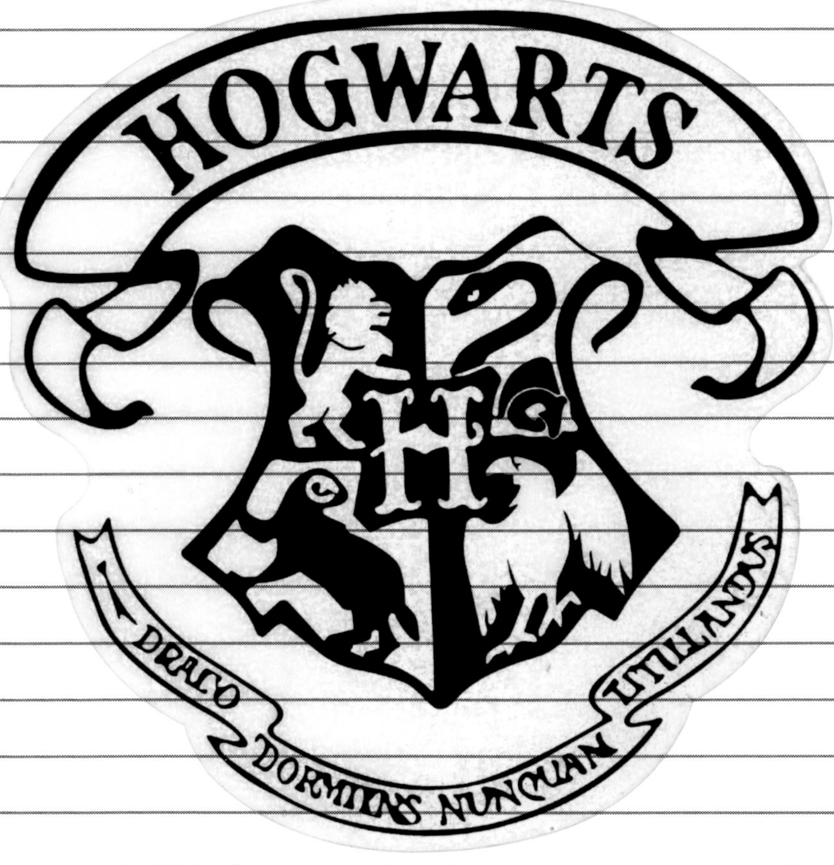
HOGWARTS
DRACO DORMIENS NUNQUAM TITILLANDUS

38829919R00057

Made in the USA
Lexington, KY
11 May 2019